# Euro Crisis

## Aggregate Demand Control is European Single Currency Weakness.

A critique of the current European economic governance system, with practical solutions.

## By

## Peter James Rhys Morgan

# Declarations.

Originally Published in April 2011 and Republished in January 2012 by Morganist Economics.

Revised in September 2018, January 2020 and October 2023.

ISBN 978-1-61364-207-8

Blog: morganisteconomics.blogspot.com

# What is Morganist Economics?

Morganist Economics is a progressive school of economic thought. Most of the current mainstream schools of economic thought tend to concentrate on the size of government, with an emphasis on whether to stimulate the economy during a downturn or not. Morganist Economics puts the emphasis on developing the tools used to control or manage the economy in a more effective less costly way.

An example of this would be a Keynesian would argue to stimulate the economy during an economic slump, a Monetarist would argue that the economy should not be stimulated and that the interest rate should be used to hit an inflation target. Whereas a Morganist would question whether the tools or mechanisms used to achieve **either** objective is beneficial to the long term economy.

Morganist Economics therefore puts innovation and the concept of the requirement of perpetual change, as the centrepiece of its thinking. As society alters through time the needs of the economy will also change so new tools and mechanisms have to be introduced to allow for the progression of social needs.

This has led to the creation of new aggregate demand controls, a new banking system and a new taxation system among other things, which are aimed at being able to deliver a pragmatic economic system that can deal with the new demands of a flexible society.

By looking at economics through a different view point and by developing these original ideas it has led to a new perspective on the failings of the current economic, banking and financial systems, which highlights the recent problems in a way other economists have failed to see.

# Table of Contents.

# Preface.

I originally wrote this book at the request of a leading British think tank, with the intention of publishing it with them. I was then asked by another leading British think tank to publish the work with them, due to their interest in the original concepts in the latter part of the book. However, I decided to self publish the work, so I did not have to compromise on the content, as both think tanks interested in publishing were intent on promoting their own unique perspectives.

By self publishing the work I maintain an outside perspective of the situation pertaining to the economic governance of the Single European Monetary system. I look at the situation purely from a macroeconomic perspective, rather than a biased opinion based on my own personal view. Both European sceptics and supporters can benefit from reading this book, to examine the limitations of the current system and the original solutions that I put forward to remedy the situation.

**Note of Interest:** Since it was originally published in 2011 this book has been included in "The Euro: Information Resources and Bibliography" list at the European University Institute (EUI).

# Summary.

This book discusses the requirements of aggregate demand for a stable economy. Closely assessing the prioritisation of the requirements, the difficulties and conflicts this creates throughout the European Union (EU). The issues addressed are then examined with the current problems within the Eurozone, which have created limitations for the European Central Bank's (ECB) ability to function. This is likely the result of the ECB's prioritisation of aggregate demand control, or the lack thereof, being different to other central banks'.

Limitations of monetary policy in controlling aggregate demand, due to high levels of debt and the difficulties of domestic fiscal policy aggregate demand controls are then explained. With an emphasis on the increasing governmental deficits throughout the EU and the impact this has on economic controls. Then some suggestions of heterodox aggregate demand control tools are discussed to evaluate whether they may work and whether they could enable recovery, if the EU member states do not have the current restrictions of the ECB.

# Aggregate demand control has four main functions.

I define aggregate demand as,

> *"The total expenditure of a nation or an economy (in nominal terms) for domestic goods and services in a set period of time."*

Aggregate demand composes of the following components; Consumer Expenditure (C), Investment Expenditure (I), Government Expenditure (G) and Net Exports (international trade exports minus imports) (NX).

Aggregate demand = C + I + G + NX.

Reference (Davies, Lowes & Pass, 2005).

Aggregate demand control has four main functions within a modern economic model.

1.) Increasing or decreasing aggregate demand for goods and labour (stimulus).
-Economic stimulus, which is an injection of money into the economy, to react to a shortage of demand in the labour market (unemployment). Or the reduction of stimulus, which takes money out of the economy, to react to an increase in demand for goods, which created high prices (inflation).
2.) Strengthening or weakening the currency.
-Maintaining one country's currency value against other currencies to sustain purchasing power.

3.) Maintaining the value of return.

-Maintaining the value of return on investments so the same level of goods can be bought from one period of time to another through sustaining portfolio value, preventing loss of wealth occurring as a result of accelerating price inflation.

4.) Maintaining the value of repayment.

-Maintaining the value of repayment on loans so that the instalments do not damage or prohibit the operations of a business, due to greater costs as a result of higher purchasing power from the existing money supply created by price deflation on goods making repayment more expensive.

The first is the primary concern at present in most central banks and is the dividing line of the schools of economic thought. The concept of controlling aggregate demand to react to labour market disequilibrium is often considered the main area of debate in economics. In such a scenario the Rational Expectations school of thought do not believe the market should be interfered with, due to the expectation the workers will find more work immediately for less pay.

This is practiced by "Inflation Targeting" when a fixed level of inflation is selected and efforts are made to prevent "Over Stimulation" of the economy, which supply side economists believe will create inflation (Bernanke, Laubach, Mishkin & Posen, 2001). The Adaptive Expectations school believe the market will rectify itself in time and may require intervention, but generally avoid it and the Keynesians believe the market needs a guiding hand through stimulus to enable employment (Stein, 1981).

# 1.) Failings of the ECB mandate.

Stimulus, or the reduction of stimulus, is only one aspect of aggregate demand control, however it is the aspect which receives the highest level of attention. Neglecting the other three functions, which are needed for a healthy economy. It is, partly, this neglect that the European Union (EU) is guilty of when it imposes a European Central Bank (ECB) that does not possess the power other central banks have. This is due to having an inflation target and limitations on the ability to stimulate through monetary policy, using techniques such as Quantitative Easing. The problem is the result of a misunderstanding of what a central bank has to perform to maintain stability. The emphasis of the ECB is to maintain the value of the Euro against other currencies in the world to encourage trade and investment, by keeping the money supply controlled. This is something which it can do and successfully, at least in the short term.

The ECB provides primary concern on a different factor to other central banks, namely the overall stability of the currency and the money supply, instead of individual member state stimulation in an attempt to address abnormalities in the labour market. It also does not pay enough attention to the value of return or the value of repayment on an individual member state level, which is reason for concern in itself. The attempts to influence individual member states' money supplies to reinforce the set objectives to enable a competitive market are inhibited by the limitations of the regulations of the ECB itself.

Below is a quote from the ECB website, explaining the primary objective of the ECB and how it is related to monetary policy control. Note that maintaining price stability also maintains currency stability and vice versa, by increasing the money supply the currency price should fall making goods cheaper for external buyers. Conversely by reducing the money supply the currency price should rise making goods more expensive for external buyers. Remember currency value represents the cost of purchasing goods within a country or economic region, thus the two are priced equivalently. This may however be different in a federal system, such as the Eurozone because each member state has its own domestic economic targets.

*"The primary objective of the ECB's monetary policy is to maintain price stability. This is the best contribution monetary policy can make to economic growth."* Data available for free at ECB website.

(ECB, www.ecb.int, 2010).

Is this assumption correct? It is a very important part of aggregate demand control, most economists would not doubt that. However this does not mean it is the most important or should receive such a high level of precedence over the other functions of monetary policy. Who is making this judgment? And what justification do they have in doing so? It is a very assumptive comment to make and base the whole working of a federal economic system on. It first assumes that to gain economic power a sustained currency value is required. Sometimes a low currency value is required to entice foreign investors and stimulate trade. Surely the ECB doctrine eliminates this possibility by setting a boundary to the devaluation of the currency.

Limitations of the Eurozone member states to control monetary targets, is also an important dimension to the argument. The high private debt levels across the EU make it difficult to alter money supply using the interest rate. If the interest rate rises the effect on the outstanding repayment obligations would damage businesses and create repossessions. Conversely if the interest rate falls, the return on the lent money is not sufficient to provide incentive to lend in the future, or in some cases to provide an income for dependents creating pensioner poverty. Taking the above consequences into consideration is it even possible for member states to control aggregate demand using monetary policy? It is an extremely limiting circumstance due to the abnormal levels of personal debt (Armitstead, 2011). The situation is further strained with a stringent inflation target of two percent.

*"In the pursuit of price stability, the ECB aims at maintaining inflation rates below, but close to, 2% over the medium term."* Data available for free at ECB website.

(ECB, www.ecb.int, 2010).

A two percent inflation target prevents the ECB from being able to devalue the currency to encourage foreign interest. Although by maintaining the currency value it solidifies the purchasing power of the Eurozone. It only addresses one economic strategy and holds an arrogant pretense that the Eurozone will always be a heavy importer and will be able to maintain full labour market equilibrium, from domestic demand almost solely. This is becoming a false view point in the current environment, as it is likely the Euro will have to weaken to compete with America and the new emerging Brazilian, Russian, Indian and Chinese (BRIC) economies. With the future potential of reduced interest in European goods and a high level of unemployment across the EU, it leads to questioning the validity of the ECB's economic assumptions.

It is also important to note this was the strategy of the Bank of England, until the cut in interest rates to half a percent and the introduction of quantitative easing (Stewart, 2009). This was implemented to increase demand for goods and labour, shifting the priority of aggregate demand control from currency stability to reaching labour market equilibrium. Is the ECB strategy correct? And if not, could it be altered to put other factors of aggregate demand control at a higher level of importance? Even if the ECB can deliver change in policy, can it achieve it without damaging member states' economies? This is something that other central banks do not have to worry about, as they only have one government and labour market to consider, unlike the ECB. This leaves the question does the ECB have the power or even the ability to enforce such a change of hierarchical importance in the structure of aggregate demand function?

The problem is when the member states in the Eurozone, which act as separate markets and have separate fiscal policies, create situations that need intervention, on the other factors aggregate demand is used to influence. For example, some member states have a higher public or private debt ratio when compared to others. Although they have their own central banks, which have their own debt functions. They are required to remain within parameters set by the ECB, to meet the Euro currency value targets. The member states are therefore limited to what action they can take, due to the ECB attempting to maintain the overall strength of the currency across the whole Eurozone. In short, the ECB has to hold currency units within set parameters, so the supply of Euros is not too high or too low, as this will affect the purchasing power of the currency. The member states' actions will impact money supply and the currency value, so control is needed.

This conflicts with the need to maintain value of return and the need to maintain value of repayment, which are affected by the money supply and value of the currency. If one member state of the Eurozone has very high inflation or deflation, the central bank will have to stay within the parameters set by the ECB. This may not enable the member state to keep the money supply within the required boundaries, to maintain the value of return or the value of repayment. The member state's inflationary or deflationary gap is not solely as a result of the money supply of the Euro, but as a result of various factors unique to each individual member state. The availability of goods in addition to taxes and fiscal policy in general will determine different prices of goods and services across the Eurozone, regardless of the international Euro value.

As a result, the ECB puts the stability of the currency before the purchasing power of individuals in member states impacting the value of their pensions, savings and the operations of businesses.

This also has implications on banking, due to the value of return being the incentive to lend and the value of repayment being the incentive to borrow. If the inflationary or deflationary gap is too great it is not cost effective to lend or borrow, depending on the circumstance, thus preventing the banking system from functioning properly. Also, one member state may have opposite requirements to the overall Euro. For example, the member state might have inflation requiring a reduction in money supply but the Euro might be too strong requiring an increase in money supply. These positions and treatments contradict each other, but currency value is prioritised.

# 2.) Individual Nation Policy.

By attempting or in fact succeeding to maintain currency value in the world markets, it has come at the cost of the ability to control member states' individual aggregate demand targets. There is some area for aggregate demand control, in the form of individual member state fiscal policy however this has been weakened with the high government deficits seen across the EU. An example of this is when governments increase spending, to create jobs in an attempt to control imbalances with the labour market. The governments' ability to spend money is diminished or no longer there due to high levels of government debt across the Eurozone, in addition to falling revenue as a result of the failing economy. The alternative is to borrow even more and hope the situation resolves itself. Then pay back the money with future taxation.

This strategy is flawed due to the already high levels of debt, acting as a disincentive to buy further government treasuries from the fear of the inability to repay them. The credit rating has also fallen in some countries making the cost of borrowing higher, due to the increased risk leading to more interest to justify lending. This situation has constrained central banks across the EU, which lost the ability to control their internal inflationary or deflationary gaps through the traditional policy mix. This in turn has an effect on the overall valuation of the Euro and its international value against other currencies.

There are other reasons why aggregate demand is difficult to control with fiscal policy. When civil servants pay is held at the same level from year to year to control inflation, unions create disruptions and governments frequently fold. A similar scenario was seen in France in 2006 with the Youth Labour Protests, when students reacted violently against proposals to introduce legislation preventing them from having the same employment safeguards that more senior members of society were entitled to. The law called the, "Loi pour l'égalité des chances", which translates to Equal Opportunity Law, attempted to introduce a new employment contract known as the, "Contrat première embauche" (CPE), which translates to First/Beginning Employment/Workers Contract.

The CPE contract would have enabled employers to terminate the employment of any member of staff under the age of twenty-six, in the first two years of their employment without any reason. The protests started on February 7th 2006, when as many as four hundred thousand students marched in one hundred and eighty-seven different protests across France. The demonstrations worsened in March and April 2006, when an estimated three point one million people were protesting and sixty-seven Universities were either blockaded or began strike action. The pressure of the social disorder resulted in the then President Jacques Chirac preventing the introduction of the CPE legislation on April 10th 2006, to appease the students and unions by meeting their demands on employment rights (Sciolino & Smith, 2006).

Protesting is a common occurrence in France, but most governments are constrained when attempting to control aggregate demand with fiscal policy due to objections and political limitations. Another example is taxation alterations or spending cuts, which put further fuel on the fire. In short fiscal policy is not a guaranteed viable alternative to monetary policy. There is not always room for change especially if the government is weak or an election is near, which is the case across most of Europe due to the current economic situation.

In addition to these limitations the ECB has insisted on further aggregate demand control restraints, with the Stability and Growth Pact (SGP). The SGP was introduced to control the fiscal forces that affect aggregate demand, in an attempt to maintain overall Euro currency value. It was adopted in 1997 and set the following criteria for member states,

Stability and Growth Pact criteria.

- *The government deficit to gross domestic product ratio cannot exceed 3%. The government debt to gross domestic product ratio cannot exceed 60%.*
- *Price stability must be maintained with an average inflation rate, to be upheld for one year before the review. The rate of inflation must not exceed one and a half percent of the three best performing Member States in regards to price stability.*
- *A long term nominal interest rate is required, it must not exceed by more than two percent the three best performing Member States in regards to price stability.*

- *Normal fluctuation margins set for the exchange rate mechanism must be regarded without disparities for a minimum of two years before the review.*

Reference (Europa, 2010).

# 3.) Indebtedness of PIIGS.

The SGP prevents the Eurozone member states from spending money in the downturn period of the economic cycle to encourage growth, by restraining government deficits, putting legal limitations on fiscal policy throughout the Eurozone. It is also interesting to point out that some of the EU member states did not, or have not, abided by the criteria. Most member states exceed the governmental debt limits. Greece in particular has defied the expectations of the SGP in addition to hiding this fact from the rest of the EU, until it was too late.

Table 1 in Appendix I shows the net income or borrowing surpluses or deficits for the Euro Area and Greece since 2000. Note how both columns are negative throughout the period with the Greek deficits exceeding the Euro Area on every occasion. Although the Greek deficits are very high in comparison to the Euro Area, it is still a reason for concern if the overall Euro Area has generated a net loss each year since its conception.

This indicates the member states in the Eurozone that have surpluses do not compensate for the excessive deficits of the highly indebted member states. How can such a union continue when there is unsustainable expenditure that is not compensated for through the dispersion of net surpluses against net deficits? It is just a matter of time before the overall debt obligation damages the creditor nations. As a result of the mismanaged member states, due to the damage it will do to the single

European currency, if the poorly managed member states deteriorate further.

Graph 1 in Appendix I is a graphical representation of Greek public sector deficits in comparison to the Euro Area public sector deficits (Eurostat, 2010). It highlights the high level of debt on a national scale in comparison to the rest of the Eurozone. But why is there such a high level of debt in Greece?

To start with there is concern over the accuracy of the collected data relating to debt across the Eurozone. Greece in particular has been investigated for its non compliance with Eurozone regulation, on the computation of national debt figures. The European Statistical System (ESS), the organisation that was set up to regulate the financial and economic statistics across the Eurozone, which is made up of Eurostat and National Statistical Institutes (NSIs), had to intervene in 2004 when it became apparent that Greece had not conformed to the regulatory framework.

It was discovered in the 2004 report that the Greek NSI had failed to comply with regulations set out in ESA 95 rules, in eleven different areas. These areas included hidden surplus costs in social security, hospitals and military expenditure among others. The report was not fully closed until 2007, when it was decided that another governing body had to be set up to ensure correct treatment of statistical data.

One reason for the need of a new regulatory body was the limitations of Eurostat, which had and still has no direct involvement in the statistical data compiled in each member state. This is the responsibility of the individual NSIs and as a result left the opportunity for creative accounting. To tackle this, the "European Statistics Code of Practice" was set in 2005 and in 2008 the European Statistical Governance Advisory Board (ESGAB) was set up to regulate the NSIs (EC, 2010).

Regardless of whether the accounting practices of the member states and the deficiency of transparency thereof were improved by the ESS's actions, what is certain is the ability of the organisation to manage the high levels of debt in Greece has not been achieved.

The European Commission (EC) did set requirements for highly indebted member states, with the Excessive Deficit Procedure (EDP), with the intention of forcing member states with large deficits to not exceed the requirements of the Stability and Growth Pact. The figures in Table 1 for the years 2008 and 2009 have grown more than any other year preceding. Indicating all efforts made by the EC to reduce debt levels in Greece failed throughout its membership in the Eurozone and indeed the Eurozone as a whole.

The situation recently worsened as Portugal, Ireland, Italy and Spain also reported trouble relating to public debt (McDowell, 2010). These countries, which along with Greece are known as the PIIGS, have all entered into austerity packages in an attempt to reduce fiscal expenditure. Table 2 in Appendix II is a log of net deficits for some other EU member states, some are Eurozone and some are non Eurozone. The figures suggest other member states may have difficulty in the future in particular Hungary, Slovakia and Malta. (NEZ is Non Eurozone).

Graph 2 in Appendix II clearly shows there is reason for concern, with the deficit levels of member states that have not publicly declared difficulty like the PIIGS member states. Indicating debt levels are higher than anticipated in the Eurozone and the wider European Union. This also assumes the figures are truly reliable and the other member states comply with the recommendations set by the ESS. If the figures are not reliable, there could be even higher liabilities than the data displays.

What is more disturbing than that is the graphical display of the data, showing that some member states have a continually high debt ratio. Although the year of peak borrowing is lower than Greece's peak borrowing, the long term average liabilities are not far off. A closer analysis of the statistics showing the mean average and standard deviation of the data is shown in Table 3 in Appendix III.

Table 3 and Graph 3 in Appendix III show worrying data. The average net liability of Greece over the time period is (- 6.1) %. There are some Eurozone member states with high average liabilities Hungary, Slovakia and Malta in particular are concerning, showing average net liabilities of (- 5.95) %, (- 4.95) % and (- 4.86) % respectively. Although they are small member states in comparison to the PIIGS, it is worrying that so many other member states are in a similar position. Further worries are highlighted by the volatility of the liabilities.

Greece has a high level of volatility relating to debt requirement, suggesting there were periods when less debt was required. This indicates the Greek economy is dependent on fiscal stimulus to encourage growth, as the changing requirement of borrowing implies it follows the ups and downs of the business cycle. As a result, the austerity package is likely to be very damaging to the Greek economy as it will now not be able to maintain the same borrowing habits to encourage growth throughout downturns.

Hungary, Slovakia and Malta are in similar positions to Greece, as they all have high levels of debt and high volatility. This suggests their economies are based on the need for fiscal stimulus to enable growth throughout the downturn periods. As a result, if Hungary, Slovakia or Malta entered into the same sovereign debt position the Greeks are currently in the outcome could become very similar.

Poland is less volatile suggesting it is not so dependent on fiscal stimulus during economic downturns. As a result, it is less likely to be in a position like the Greek economy although it is still a strain on the wider EU and more responsible member states. If the ECB wishes to avoid further deterioration of the Eurozone, it should act now to prevent these other member states from entering a sovereign debt crisis.

# 4.) Can Quantitative Easing work?

It is now evident the extent of government debt across the Eurozone and the European Union as a whole, is at a level where fiscal policy cannot be used to control aggregate demand. This has led some central banks such as the Bank of England to resort to Quantitative Easing (Stewart, 2009), which is the expansion of the money supply to attempt to increase aggregate demand (Buiter, 2008). This is an unpopular tool and is criticised for creating inflationary pressure, later on in the business cycle (Dixon & Hadas, 2009).

Unfortunately, it also disrupts the ECB's primary concern on the stability of currency value as a result of this potential fear of inflation. It also assumes the tool will be useful. Is there any justification to suggest the increase of money supply will lead to a recovery in the long term? Even if it is successful, does the ECB possess the power to direct the tool effectively across the member states to eliminate each of their unique economic problems?

This is something difficult to expect, when you take into consideration the primary aim of the ECB was to control currency value. Pursuing such a change in policy would be an admission of the institution's failure to deliver on its original strategy. Does this not indicate the ECB has failed by not reaching its own aim? Why would such an institution be put in a position of control, when it has not succeeded in the past?

In any event it suggests the ECB does not have the power to control aggregate demand, for the required reasons the member states need it to under these circumstances, if it ever really did. Was the primary concern of the ECB just a cover up excuse, to hide the inadequacy to deliver effective federalised aggregate demand control?

If the ECB uses quantitative easing to inflate the Euro to help pay for the debts of the failing member states of the Eurozone, it could mean a wealth transfer from the more successful member states that do not receive the payments depending on how it is applied. Each member state would have different requirements, some would require more stimulus than others.

An increase in the Euro's money supply to provide stimulus to the ailing economies, would devalue the currency for every member state. If the investment of the extra funds was not distributed evenly, it would transfer wealth as the purchasing power of the lesser funded member states would have diminished. As the countries that are in the worst situation would be the main benefactors, it would be rewarding failure.

It would put pressure on the more successful member states and might act as a force for them to leave the EU. Even if it is not at the governmental level, as the economic situation deteriorates, the mass populace is likely to become weary of the economic damage the monetary union is creating and put pressure on the government to leave.

Further pressure arises from the cost of membership of the EU and the likelihood it will increase, even for none Eurozone member states, to support the struggling Eurozone. This is an important point to make as the cost of EU membership is high for countries like the UK, which has already raised questions as to whether it should remain a member.

If the cost increases further the political case for remaining in the EU is weakened. Also, when you take into consideration the main argument at the moment for the UK to be in the EU is trade. If the Euro weakens and the EU economy further deteriorates, it becomes a less powerful position to uphold in political debate.

The opposition of the UK towards the EU became more apparent recently when the British Prime Minister, David Cameron, vetoed the new EU treaty intended to resolve the economic crisis on 9th December 2011 (Hewitt, 2011). The UK was the only member, of the twenty-seven EU member states, to veto the accord. The implementation of the new treaty was seen by many as a power grab by the EU, due to it pushing for a closer fiscal union between the member states (Euronews, 2011).

# 5.) Advantages of Independent Currency.

In addition to the political issues the situation creates being in the single currency takes away natural compensations, relating to sovereign debt repayments that were available to the member state when it had its own currency. For example, if Greece had its own currency there would be certain compensations against economic downturn. One example of this relates to the international demand for Greek goods. If the output of the Greek economy slows down one way to get out of recession is to increase the level of external demand.

If Greece was able to devalue its own currency by increasing money supply through "seigniorage", it would increase the demand and investment from foreign entities due to the low costs in real terms. Also, the labour force would become more desirable as the willingness to work and for less money is created through economic hardship. As the Euro is based on the overall value of the monetary units across the Eurozone, the Greek relationship with economic forces is altered by being in the Eurozone. In short, the Greek government cannot use the "seigniorage" or "quantitative easing" techniques to entice economic growth due to the single European currency and the objective of maintaining currency value.

Although the above comments have been made previously in this paper, but applied to the Eurozone as a whole, there is a deeper dimension regarding this issue. As repayments of loans relate to the purchasing value of the currency, any inflationary or deflationary gap will have an effect on the relationship with the investor. Due to Greece being highly indebted and having to pay enormous amounts of debt back with interest, this relationship becomes exacerbated. If there is deflation the relative repayments become higher and could cause economic damage. The converse is also true if inflation occurs the repayment is diminished in real terms (Begg, Dornbusch & Fischer, 2003).

This adds greater emphasis to the point raised above, in relation to the limitations of monetary control as a result of being in the Euro. However, even if the Greek government did not increase the money supply, there would be a natural compensation if the economy deteriorated. If the output declined and the money supply stayed at the same level, it would create a supply shock resulting in an inflationary gap. This inflationary gap would reduce the repayment cost of the debt, in real terms the situation is the same. As the Euro is based on the overall Eurozone stability this natural compensation is unlikely to occur, due to the reduction in output not being directly offset by a domestic currency. Creating an environment where the Greek repayment costs could increase in real terms.

What makes the situation perhaps more serious is rather than this natural inflationary compensation occurring due to the relationship with the Euro, it could make it worse. If the Euro moves in the wrong direction and increases in value there could be a deflationary gap, which would make the repayments even more expensive pushing Greece's economy into an even worse position. Although this may be unlikely there is a possibility of it happening and even if it was only for a short period, it could do irreversible damage.

# 6.) Problems with the Bailout.

Another limitation of aggregate demand control in the Eurozone and the EU as a whole is the Greek bailout and the potential bailout of other Eurozone member states. The PIIGS in particular pose an enormous threat, although as shown previously in this paper the danger across the EU as a whole is wider than first thought. If the bailout extends further the investment of other Eurozone member states to prop up the failing member states, through the ECB will increase.

This is demonstrated with the compounded deficits of other member states, especially in the former "Eastern Bloc" region of the EU. The bailout and the austerity requirements have a detrimental effect on the sustainability of aggregate demand, due to the tightening of fiscal policy. However, if the bailout was not given aggregate demand would have fallen anyway. Perhaps neither, the bailout or allowing the member state to default will provide a solution and any intervention or the lack of it is already too late.

The danger of the Greek bailout and other potential bailouts, across the Eurozone could impair the ability of the ECB to control aggregate demand. It is therefore important to investigate the intricate details that led to the Greek sovereign debt crisis. It is already acknowledged that Greece has hidden debt liabilities, through inaccurate statistical representation and that the debt level has compounded over the last decade, since records began.

One main issue is the cost of debt repayment, which rose on the 27th April 2010 when Standard & Poor's the credit rating agency downgraded Greek bonds to "Junk Status". The ten-year bond yield rose to 10% and the two-year bond yield rose to almost 15%, which is the highest level ever recorded in the Eurozone. It also brings the Greek bond risk classification into the same category as Azerbaijan, Colombia and Romania (Tyldesley, 2010).

Greece was not the only casualty. Portugal was also downgraded by two classifications, to A- by Standard & Poor's, on the same day. The Portuguese two-year bond yield increased by 1.07% from 4.16% to 5.23%, creating a shockwave across European stock markets. The FTSE 100 closed down 2.6%, with the German Dax falling by 2.7% and the French Cac 40 losing 3.8% of its value by the market close (BBC, 2010).

These higher repayments on the outstanding sovereign debt obligations put further strain on the Greek government, which was already pressured as a result of an urgent payment on an outstanding debt of €8.5 Billion (£7.3 Billion) paid on the 19th May 2010. The Greek government had to request the financial aid of the other Eurozone members states, to fund the immediate debt repayment. Germany took the leading role and agreed to make the required payment, which had now risen as a result of the downgrading of Greek bonds (Heritage, 2010).

In addition to the emergency €8.5 Billion loan Greece requested a Stand-by Arrangement of a further €26.4 Billion over a three-year period, with the intention of supporting future economic growth. This consisted of a €4.8 Billion first payment, with the remainder being paid in twelve instalments over the three-year period. The fund is overseen by the EC, ECB and International Monetary Fund (IMF) with a 3:8 ratio of the funds coming from the IMF, the remaining "bulk" of the financing is to be made by the other 17 Eurozone member states.

The payment of each member state is dependent on the ratio of the shares each member state owns in the ECB, the higher the number of shares the higher the expected funding. Greece is required to repay the loan, which carries a high interest charge including a 0.5% initial service charge on each drawing. The interest payable is based on a floating spread of 3 percentage points, however if the three-year period is exceeded the spread percentage increases to 4 percentage points (IMF, 2010).

Unfortunately, the sovereign debt crisis magnified the existing problems in the private sector which is on the edge of a banking crisis. To avoid such an outcome the European Financial Stability Fund was set up with €440 Billion available to prevent private sector banking default (Armitstead, 2011). Liquidity pressures have led to the extension of government support facilities (IMF, 2010).

One such support facility is the suspension of the application of the minimum credit rating threshold in the collateral eligibility requirements, issued by the government, which was enforced by the ECB. It is hoped these measures will prevent a private sector liquidity crisis, which could start bank runs and hysteria. This could be heightened as a result of inaccurate reporting in the media, which was seen in the UK when the run on Northern Rock ensued (Congdon, 2009).

The recent crisis at Belgian Bank Dexia, which had to be bailed out by the Belgian, French and Luxembourg governments, saw the first impact of the sovereign debt crisis on the private banking sector. Banks such as Dexia, which are highly exposed to sovereign debt risk, have seen huge losses from investments in the PIIGS member states' government bonds. This has led to an inability to repay creditors and falling share prices in the financial sector, hurting investors' pockets and damaging pension funds (Peston, 2011).

Not only has the sovereign debt crisis spread to the private sector, but now it has spread to the stronger member states in the Eurozone. France has been brought into the crisis through its exposure to the PIIGS member states' sovereign debt. It was announced on 13th January 2012, by Standard & Poor's ratings agency, that France's credit rating would be downgraded from AAA to AA+. Austria was also downgraded from AAA to AA+, due to its exposure to Eastern European debt (BBC, 2012). This indicates all efforts made so far to resolve the Eurozone debt crisis have been ineffective, as it has continued to spread further.

# 7.) Problems of Greece.

This adds to the cost of preventing Greek default cumulating in a total of $300 Billion at present, which is around 100% of Greek GDP, although the cost may rise in the future (Schuman, 2011). The funding provided has only been agreed on the terms that the Greek government concedes to a stringent austerity package. This package includes the reduction in the number of public holidays, public sector workers, pension payments, military forces and defence spending to name only a few cuts.

In addition, attempts to increase public revenue to make debt repayments have been set in motion including a rise in the already high rate of VAT from 21% to 23% for the higher rate and 10% to 11% for the lower rate. It is expected that the rise in VAT will increase revenue by 2.1% of GDP, which when combined with other taxation measures will generate 4% of GDP in additional revenue.

Higher taxation raises issues with the ability to repay the money lent. Arguments have been made in favour of reducing taxation to encourage growth in an economy. An increase in taxation to raise government revenue could have the opposite effect to the expected outcome. It is also important to point out that Greece borrowed money creating this situation in the first place, which indicates there may be a reason for it taking such action. One suggestion is that the private sector in Greece is constrained requiring fiscal stimulus to enter recovery.

This view is supported with evidence earlier in this paper that showed Greece has a volatile borrowing history and a high standard deviation. This means Greece borrows more money at certain times, suggesting a requirement of capital during the downturns in the business cycle. Assuming this is accurate it indicates the private sector is indeed constrained. This leads to the question, why is the Greek private sector unable to flourish without public sector provisions?

Greece has one of the worst aging demographics in Europe. It is expected that there will be a rise in government costs of 12.5% by the year 2050, as a result. In addition, a 4.5% increase in healthcare expenditure is anticipated due to the strain of the aging population. Infrastructure is also counterproductive for small and medium business growth, as the market is largely made up of monopolies and oligopolies who own the majority of facilities.

A large military for a long period of time has led to the limitation of labour market skills, which enable the private sector to grow. Poor exports leading to a negative balance of payments is evidence the private sector is not capable of competing with foreign opposition. The imbalance has worsened in recent years, in January 2010 it was announced by the Bank of Greece that there was an increase of 9.7% in the deficit of the balance of payments from the previous year creating a $5.05 Billion disparity (MENAFN, 2010).

It is projected by the IMF that exports will grow over the next year by 22.6% (IMF, 2010), which seems optimistic to say the least. Other projections of growth by the IMF seem unrealistic, as a result of the worsening economic environment across the rest of the EU and global market as a whole. With the position of foreign markets weakening, it is difficult to see how such a large increase in growth can be expected.

The IMF's predictions for unemployment rates throughout the next few years seem more realistic, with a rise from 9.4% in 2009 to 13.4% in 2015 seeing a peak of 14.8% in 2012. The figures remain high throughout the period. This is counter projective, as it is difficult to anticipate any form of growth when unemployment is rising. Further concern is raised by the estimation Greece will not start reducing its deficit till 2013, at which time the public sector liability will peak at 150% of GDP (IMF, 2010).

All estimates assume the global market will remain stable and there will not be any kind of market shock impacting the Greek economy. However, it is important to note the difficulties the global economy is encountering as a result of the fallout of the subprime defaults and the actions of governments and central banks. The UK in particular took drastic action to resolve the panic in the wake of the "Credit Crunch" (Grice, 2009).

This action and the potential long term ramifications have been criticised suggesting the cure might be worse than the disease (Congdon, 2009). In any event record liabilities have been accrued by governments across the World and Europe in particular, in the name of financial stability. Whether this is attained or not is questionable. What is certain is the constraint this will have on private sector growth, especially when the task of repaying the cost of bailouts is implemented which usually takes the form of tax increases. Is there a way out for the EU member states?

# 8.) Nation State Solutions.

If the member states could control aggregate demand individually to meet their own requirements, there is the potential they could resolve their domestic economic problems. As the orthodox avenues of aggregate demand control have been exhausted, are there alternatives that could be used without constraints or limitations?

# A.) Could pension saving be used to control aggregate demand?

One alternative is controlling aggregate demand through saving, but using a different mechanism to regulate it. Rather than the interest rate mechanism altering to change saving habits, the pension system could be altered to entice saving or encourage spending. This could be done on an incentive based model or a mandatory model, leading to a new dimension to the policy mix.

By increasing or decreasing monthly pension contributions the saving rate would be managed transparently, with the ability to observe and delicately change saving and spending habits. Another advantage, unlike tax or interest, would be the money taken out of the transaction period is given back to the individual on retirement. Note the pension pot is not tampered with the contributions are simply higher or lower depending on the related need. Over time the disparity is compensated with the peaks and troughs seen in the business cycle providing a pension.

The volume of pension saving is substantial and just a small alteration in the monthly contribution/payment, could increase or decrease inflationary pressure. It would work in a similar way to the interest rate mechanism, which is reviewed monthly and usually consists of small alterations in the cost of lending of as little as a quarter of a percent.

The effect of the interest rate alteration is then monitored and scrutinised by the Bank of England, over a two-year period. This process is called the, "Transmission Mechanism" and enables the Bank of England to make decisions on future actions regarding interest rate changes (George, 2003).

It is possible to use pension saving to achieve the same function of the interest rate mechanism, in regards to aggregate demand control. Nearly £7 billion was claimed by employees in pension tax relief in 2009/2010, within the UK. Even if they were all paying forty percent tax on all of those contributions, the amount saved in employee pension contributions alone in that year was at least £17.5 billion.

In addition to this amount employers saved £13.68 billion in pension contributions. This suggests that the annual pension saving total is £31.18 billion (HM Revenue & Customs, 2010). Of course, there is no limit on how much people can save so the potential saving could be one hundred percent of income or zero percent of income in theory. This would definitely have an effect on inflationary or deflationary pressure.

It does however indicate the level of aggregate demand can be changed effectively by using pension contributions as a saving mechanism, without having a severe impact on an individual's life style. On an individual level it could be achieved by encouraging or demanding a small increase or decrease on a monthly pension contribution. A sum as small as £15 more or less in each individual's pension payment from one month to another, could have the same effect as a quarter percent interest rate change on GDP.

Also, unlike interest rate alterations where the amount of money introduced or taken out of the economy is estimated the figures in regards to pension saving can be a set amount or at least immediately quantified by the administrators of pension schemes. This increases the level of transparency and reduces the cost of administering the estimation of the impact of aggregate demand controls. In short it could eliminate the need for the transmission mechanism.

There are two ways that pension saving with the intention of controlling aggregate demand could be implemented on an operational level. One is through incentives, which already exists in the form of tax reliefs and could be expanded upon to encourage or discourage pension saving. The other is through mandatory contributions, which exists on different levels throughout the EU and already operates in some member states.

In 1987 the International Association for the Study of Insurance Economics set up a research programme called the "Four Pillars", which identifies the four ways in which countries base pension funding, with the aim of providing solutions to the shortfall in expected pension income (IASIE, 1987). The four pillars are as follows,

> *1. Pillar – Compulsory state pensions.*
> *2. Pillar – Occupational pensions.*
> *3. Pillar – Individual savings.*
> *4. Pillar – Extending work life.*

Reference (IASIE, 1987).

It is important to note that although it is only the first pillar which is compulsory, many countries are adopting or considering making second pillar supplementary occupational pension schemes mandatory. Pioneering this reform is Hungary, which introduced obligatory second pillar pension contributions in 1998 (Investors, 2010). The modifications very closely followed the World Bank's model for pension reform and many other European countries including Bulgaria, Estonia, Latvia, Lithuania, Poland, Romania, Slovakia and Slovenia have used Hungary as a precedent for their own reforms.

The Czech Republic was the only Eastern European member state not to introduce radical reforms, although they intend to launch pension reforms in 2013 (Dunai, 2010). There is currently no compulsory requirement for employers to make pension contributions to an occupational pension scheme in the UK. However, there is a requirement for employers to make a stakeholder pension scheme accessible if they employ five or more members of staff (Leigh, 2010).

Perhaps the second pillar supplementary occupational pension could be used for aggregate demand control. This could be changed on a monthly basis to force extra or reduced pension saving. This would be ideal in the UK where additional pension saving may be required to fill the pension shortfall, but is not currently legally required.

If mandatory occupational pension schemes were introduced, they could be altered on a monthly basis to manipulate inflationary or deflationary pressure and could prove very effective in both providing better pension provision and controlling aggregate demand.

Currently there is an option to make additional monthly payments on a voluntary basis to private or occupational pension schemes, these contributions are called "Additional Voluntary Contributions" or AVCs (TPAS, 2010). A similar scheme could be used to force pension saving on a mandatory basis, "Additional Mandatory Contributions" or AMCs could be introduced.

One thing that has been neglected by governments across the EU and the rest of the World for that matter, is the impact that current pension saving has on aggregate demand. It may even have a counteracting impact on the currently used methods of aggregate demand control and this may not be acknowledged, fully, by the administrators of the existing inflationary or deflationary controls.

It was stated earlier that the UK has in excess of £30 billion worth of pension saving each year. This saving has a dampening effect on aggregate demand and will reduce prices of goods. This may be a useful effect to take advantage of in other (inflationary) circumstances. But with a global deflationary gap and an emerging currency war on the way in a bid to win foreign demand, such high pension saving may not be desirable (Rahman, 2010).

In addition to this deterrent to save there are low rates of return on investments due to the loosening of monetary policy requiring low interest rates, in an effort to close the global deflationary gap. As a result, it may not be in the individual's best interest to save in the current environment due to negative real returns on saving. Since the credit crunch started in late 2007 and early 2008, there has been an increase in pension tax relief within the UK.

Suggesting that investors are looking to compensate for lost investment returns through pension tax relief. As pension tax relief is not a fixed amount, the potential bill of such an action could result in a huge liability for governments that do not limit or reduce pension saving. If the government froze pension tax relief or stopped it for a small period of time, perhaps a couple of years, it would help to increase domestic demand.

It could also prevent a huge governmental liability and provide funds to cut the national deficit without having an impact on employment. The immediate shortfall in pension saving could be deferred to a later date, when there is inflation and greater pension saving is desired to dampen demand, compensating for the previously lower contributions.

There are other advantages of using pension saving to control aggregate demand, which include the exclusion of the connection between the aggregate demand control and the lending and borrowing facility. Pension saving would not impact the return or repayment costs to lenders or borrowers respectively.

But it does maintain their value by controlling inflation and deflation. It provides the pros without the cons of other aggregate demand controls. This will reduce business failure and minimise default risk providing a stable loanable fund market. There are other ways to control aggregate demand too. They, however require a more sensitive introduction.

The other alternatives work on the concept of the velocity of money, which I define as,

> *"The speed or rate money is exchanged in an economy during a specific period of time."*

Reference (Davies, Lowes & Pass, 2005).

One example of this is liquidity efficiency, which is now explained.

# B.) The efficiency of liquidity.

One of the main economic topics argued on a regular basis is, whether a higher level of money supply will increase the level of output. This is an important debate, as it will determine the economic strategy of the government or organisation that is in charge of the economic controls of the country. One major aspect of money supply is liquidity and there are many different definitions of liquidity throughout finance. The macroeconomic definition is an area of debate in its own right. For example, David Longworth, Deputy Governor of the Bank of Canada, identifies three different types of liquidity within finance,

*1.) Macroeconomic liquidity.*

*2.) Market liquidity.*

*3.) Balance sheet liquidity.*

Reference (Agrawal, 2008).

The one constant in the three definitions is the speed at which assets can be turned into cash. For the purpose of this paper liquidity is, in macroeconomic terms, defined as,

*"The volume of assets which can be readily used within an economy to make transactions during a specific period of time."*

The efficiency of liquidity is defined as,

*"The most effective allocation/distribution of the assets/money which are/is readily available to expend within an economy to enable the highest number of transactions during a specific period of time."*

It is important to address whether liquidity itself can be made more efficient. If liquidity can become more efficient then surely the methods that are used to increase and decrease the level of liquidity are as important as the initial decision, which is what level of money supply should there be? If liquidity can become more efficient depending on the methods that are used to increase it is there the potential to make the economy produce the same level of output with a reduced level of money supply, by using the more efficient liquidity increasing methods as an alternative to the less efficient liquidity increasing methods?

As stated previously in this paper, some economists believe that the higher the level of money supply the higher the level of output. In short, they believe a greater number of monetary currency units in the economy will increase the level of resources the economy produces. However other economists believe the amount the economy produces will not be affected by the level of money supply.

Their first argument in regards to whether the increased levels of money supply will lead to a greater level of transactions is mainly supported by the view that even if people have more money, it does not mean that they will spend that money. This is a fair assumption. Just because an individual has a greater ability to purchase goods does not mean that they will purchase them.

They might choose to save the extra money an increase in money supply has created.

Increases in saving often occur when money supply increases within an economy, even for poorer people. This may happen because of a lack of confidence in the economy, which often arises at the same time money supply increases. This may be as a result of government actions to attempt to increase economic growth during a recession, by increasing money supply often referred to as "Pump Priming" which I define as,

*"An effort to stimulate economic growth within an economy through making alterations to monetary policy, fiscal policy or other means."*

Reference (Investopedia, 2010).

When governments take these actions, it indicates the economy is in trouble and as a result people are likely to save more to protect themselves in an uncertain future. When people choose to save rather than spend or they are paying down debt there is a reduction in liquidity, as the number of available assets that can be used to make transactions within the economy have reduced.

This is often called leakage. Leakage also occurs in other circumstances, such as when the cost of borrowing increases or the level of tax increases. These are the two main factors that are used by governments to increase and decrease the level of liquidity through monetary policy and fiscal policy. This was expressed by the Keynesian, "Leakages from the circular flow of income" model (Branson, 1989). I define leakage as,

*"Uses of income which do not generate a further extension of incomes."*

Reference (Black, Hashimzade & Myles, 2009).

The above definition describes leakage as part of the circular flow of income, which states money is injected into the economy as well as taken out. Control of the money supply is made possible by reaching an effective relationship between these two factors. The "Neoclassical" perspective would argue that money never leaves the economy, but is transformed and used in another way (Nadeau, 2008).

For example, money saved will later be money lent. The saved money has an impact on spending and will become part of the economy again when it is later lent out. The money does not disappear it is simply taken out of the transaction period during that time to later re-enter the economy. Whether the money is taken out of the economy in entirety or just temporarily it has a negative effect on consumer demand, which in turn impacts prices. Therefore, for the purpose of this paper leakage will refer to a reduction of money supply during a specific period of time.

An important point to make in regards to leakage is whether alterations in taxation and interest rates create leakage. Some economists (Neoclassical) argue that if a person is taxed the money will return to the economy through government spending. Therefore, it will not impact the economy if there is a greater level of taxation.

Although usually when governments tax more it is for a reason, which is often to pay off debt. If there is a high level of debt the taxation generated would not necessarily be invested back in the domestic economy through government expenditure, especially if the debt originated from abroad. This would potentially take the money out of the economy permanently.

In regards to the interest rate, when it increases people save more money. This money will then be lent out by the bank to someone else in the economy, reintroducing the money into the economy just like how the money taken in taxation is reintroduced. Therefore, the argument is self defeating as no matter what method is used to take money out of the economy the money will be returned. The effect of taking money out of the economy to reduce consumer consumption is to reduce the level of transactions, which occur during a specific period of time. Regardless of what method is used to do this.

Now that it has been established the general perception is all of the forms of increasing or decreasing the level of liquidity only create temporary lags or drags in the money that is circulating in the economy, regardless of whether that is due to a compensating injection or removal of money or the transformation of money, it is important to address which is the most beneficial type of liquidity. It would therefore be logical to select the methods of increasing liquidity that have the lowest levels of leakage. In short, the most efficient methods of increasing liquidity will be the methods that are likely to create the highest levels of consumption.

The most efficient form of increasing liquidity is unfortunately borrowing. This is due to the simple fact that people get loans to spend the money. People will almost always spend all of the money they borrow or they would not have borrowed it in the first place, because they will have to repay the principal amount back with interest and would lose money by over borrowing.

This makes borrowing a very efficient form of liquidity. The down side to this form of liquidity is the long term consequence on the economy. One day the loan will have to be paid back and the interest on the loan will also affect the quantity of the monetary currency in the economy. The other method of increasing liquidity in an economy is reducing taxation.

If the level of taxation is reduced the amount of monetary currency that can circulate in the economy will increase. However, depending on who receives these taxation reductions and their propensity to save there is the potential for future leakage. Therefore, it is possible to conclude that tax reductions are more efficient when the individuals who have the lowest propensity to save receive them.

Although there is no guarantee the individuals who receive the tax reductions will spend the extra money they receive. It is clear that the efficiency of this method of increasing liquidity can be made greater by giving those with the higher propensity to consume the tax reductions. However, the economists who do not believe a higher level of liquidity will increase the level of output would argue that although the level of money supply might have increased it does not mean that the level of output will.

The "Supply Side" concept of economics is followed by the Neoclassical, Ricardian and Austrian schools of thought, although they differ slightly in their opinions. Austrians for example believe the markets will rectify the abnormalities for the prices of goods on their own, without intervention. The Ricardians and the Monetarists attempt to reach an inflation target using monetary policy almost solely (Branson, 1989).

These perspectives first gained popularity with the "Quantity Theory of Money", which was developed further by economists after the concept of Say's Law, where it is claimed the production of goods creates its own demand (no stimulus is required), devised by 18th century economist Jean-Baptiste Say (Ajuzie, 2008). The concept of supply side economics later became popular in the 1970s after the post war dominance of Keynesian "Demand Side" economics, as a result of the Expectations Augmented Phillips Curve and Barro on the Ricardian Equivalence Theory (Barro, 1996).

It was argued that the higher level of stimulus during that period was not increasing output as Keynes' work claimed, but instead led to inflation. However, some Neo-Keynesian economists, such as Thomas Palley, argue the inflation seen in the 1970s was the result of a shortage of goods rather than the ineffectiveness of governmental stimulus (Palley, 2007).

Although the supply side economists might argue. An economy can only produce so much in a certain period and that the greater level of demand for these finite goods will only increase the price consumers will have to pay for them, as there would be an increased level of demand for the same, limited, quantity available. This conclusion creates new arguments in regards to how an economy is structured. For example, an economy and its output are not just made up of physical finite goods but services and international trade.

Service orientated economies will be able to increase output by producing more services. It therefore seems naïve for someone to say that in a highly service structured economy increases in the level of consumption would not create a higher demand for services, unless there is no unemployment in the economy. A greater level of demand would create new jobs and services increasing output.

In addition to this point if there is a service provider in an economy, for example a consultant of some kind. If they only have a level of demand to work four days a week and suddenly the level of transactions in the economy increases, the amount of demand for their service increases. They can now work five days a week and the economy would have increased its output. Therefore, if there are people who work part time and are willing to work full time. It is possible that an increase in consumer consumption will increase their workload and as a result increase the overall output of the economy.

Also, if the number of goods created within an economy are finite. Why would there be surpluses of agricultural goods stored in Butter Mountains and Wine Lakes? Surely the level of output could increase if there are more transactions and a higher level of consumer consumption, if there is unemployment and surpluses of goods?

Although admittedly if there are surpluses of goods then it means the economy is creating more than it needs, which would indicate increased liquidity is not needed to produce a higher level of output. It also means the resources the economy has are not being invested in the correct area. The investment, which has been used to create the surpluses should be used in other areas to make the economy more efficient.

Now that the concept of liquidity efficiency has been explained, it is time to investigate the practical applications that it could create. A good example is needed for this practice investigation. So, let's say that the economy has been healthy for the last six years and that aggregate supply and aggregate demand have maintained a relationship near to equilibrium throughout and as a result inflation has been continually low (see Diagram 1 Appendix IV).

Now suppose that the economy is heading for a downturn. The economy has suffered one quarter of negative growth and a second is likely to occur, which would officially be a recession. The level of aggregate supply has fallen sharply, but the level of aggregate demand has stayed the same (see Diagram 2 Appendix IV).

The output of the economy is reducing, which would indicate unemployment is rising and an inflationary gap has occurred. In this situation it is clear that a downturn has begun to occur. There are two techniques used to resolve this situation, either reduce the level of aggregate demand (tax rise or interest rate rise) or increase the level of aggregate supply by stimulating growth (tax reduction or interest rate reduction).

Unfortunately, both methods have downsides the first a reduction in aggregate demand will mean the economy will have a new equilibrium. Admittedly there will be no inflation, but it will come at the cost of a lower level of output. The second is an increase in aggregate demand used to stimulate the level of growth, however this might create an even greater inflationary gap. Is there an alternative to these two methods?

In short could liquidity become more efficient, creating a higher level of aggregate demand to stimulate a greater level of aggregate supply without producing an inflationary gap? This is the first of two points. The first which previously explained how in a service economy with unemployment, underemployment or if goods are not finite, an increase in aggregate demand does not necessarily create inflationary pressure.

By increasing aggregate demand, depending on how it is done it can create an increase in output without generating an inflationary gap. This is the point, which was looked at earlier in the paper. The level of aggregate demand does not determine inflation. Inflation is determined by the price rise in a basket of goods and services from one period of time to another. Aggregate supply and aggregate demand in Diagram 1 and Diagram 2 show the relationship in a retrospective position.

If there is a rise in aggregate demand relative to aggregate supply, it indicates a rise in prices **but it does not guarantee it**. Due to how that extra demand in real terms is utilized, it determines how the price for the basket of goods and services alters. In theory you could have an increase in aggregate demand and a simultaneous reduction in inflation, depending on the spending and saving habits of the population or the structure of the economy, although this is very unlikely.

The second point relates to how this technique of controlling liquidity to manipulate inflationary pressure can be a powerful tool. Instead of having to alter interest rates or rates of taxation you could simply change the distribution of taxation to meet the inflationary targets. This prevents the fallout of a change in the cost of borrowing or the need for fiscal changes, which are often difficult (Krugman & Obstfeld, 2003).

This could be useful now, due to monetary policy and fiscal policy being constrained. It is expected there will be a global deflationary gap in the near future (Jones, 2010). If the distribution of liquidity changed, it could close the deflationary gap (see Diagram 3 Appendix IV).

Diagram 3 shows a theoretical deflationary gap, when the level of aggregate demand falls creating a decline in the need for output. This could be countered with a redistribution of liquidity. The practical application is now explained. As explained earlier in this paper, a reduction in tax for the less affluent members of society would create more transactions for the same level of liquidity that the more affluent members would create. Please look at Appendix V for the practical example.

This is another example of how EU member states can control aggregate demand, this time using the velocity of money. Another possibility is making the leaked money in the economy easier to get back into the function of transaction. This is now explained.

# C.) The fortification of demand.

Aggregate demand is determined by the number of monetary units expended within an economy during a set period of time, "The Function of Transaction Period", used to purchase goods and services. Methods of controlling aggregate demand merely take out or put in monetary units for the function of transaction for a period of time. An example being the interest rate mechanism which will increase or decrease saving.

The saved money will re-enter the function of transaction when it is lent out to borrowers. The decrease in aggregate demand is created by the temporary absence of the money during the function of transaction period. The other aspect to altering demand with the interest rate is the cost of borrowing. The more money borrowed the greater the number of monetary units during the function of transaction period.

An increase in offered lending, as a result of a lower rate of interest, will encourage borrowing. The converse will have the opposite result. This aspect of interest rate control also works on the function of transaction. As the lower interest rate merely incentivises investment to go to credit rather than another market, which also provides funding for businesses and individuals. Thus, the increase or decrease in demand is created by a rise or fall in the number of monetary units for the function of transaction period.

The same result is attained with the taxation mechanism of aggregate demand control. An alteration in taxation will likely change the level of demand. If taxation rises the government will take in greater revenue, which they can then invest in the economy. The reduction in aggregate demand is generated by the decline in monetary units for the function of transaction period, which occurs between when the tax is taken and then later spent by the government.

Both, monetary and fiscal, policies work on the principle of leakage. Meaning the money taken out of the economy for a period of time reduces aggregate demand. There is, however, another element to the relationship that has not been looked upon. The ability for the money taken out of the function of transaction to be reintroduced, as the period the money is taken out of the function of transaction is as important as the period the money is included within the function of transaction. In short, the easier it is to get the money that is out of the function of transaction back into the function of transaction the higher the level of aggregate demand will be. The sustainability of demand is also improved and so is the availability of funding, conversely the opposite is true.

This suggests that the level of aggregate demand can be controlled by the way the money not included in the function of transaction period is used. For example, if the money saved during a period of high interest rates is used to purchase foreign debt that cannot be paid back until a set period of time in the future. It is not easily put back into the function of transaction period within the domestic economy.

It is being used in another country to increase their demand for that period of time. Thus, if the government provided incentives or restricted certain types of investment it could control aggregate demand in this manner. Although this concept has been touched upon by the transmission mechanism, it has not been pursued to control aggregate demand in itself.

It has also not been viewed as a way of making aggregate demand control superior, by not having the detrimental consequences interest rate or taxation alterations have on the economy. It can control the level of aggregate demand without conflicting on another factor of the economy. Such as enabling the ability to produce output or provide a saving return, as an income for pensioners (Brealey & Myers, 2003).

The emphasis of this type of control of aggregate demand is the isolation of the most "Fluid" investments. Fluidity relating to the ease at which the money invested can be put back into the function of transaction. The most fluid money is likely to be in private individual current accounts, then small business current accounts, then larger business current accounts, then higher rate saving accounts etc. The list would go on until it went to overseas long term bonds, which are the least fluid investments. By intervening with how and also where money is "held", control of fluidity can be achieved. Similar to Qualitative Easing.

I define Qualitative Easing as,

*"A shift in composition of the central bank's assets in the direction of less liquid and higher risk assets, maintaining a constant balance sheet size."*

Reference (Buiter, 2008).

However, the mechanism that is used to alter aggregate demand through Qualitative Easing is the composition of the debt relating to risk. This differs from Demand Fortification, which relates to the speed of the re-entry of the money that is not being used to make transactions. A similar mechanism, relating to the speed of money reintroduction has been used in the past by the Federal Reserve in America during the 1960s.

The application of the concept was called, "Operation Twist" which consisted of the Federal Reserve buying long term Treasury bonds and selling short term Treasury bonds. This reduced the duration of lending, in an effort to reintroduce assets to the function of transaction (Beckhart, 1972). Unfortunately, this proved unsuccessful according to the research conducted during its application (Zaretsky, 2008).

One suggestion as to why this failed and perhaps why Demand Fortification may work, is the lack of understanding of the use of the money when it is saved or "held". When the Federal Reserve introduced "Operation Twist", they only changed the duration of the debt they did not change the form of debt. There is no reason why the individual or entity who purchased the "new" short term debt would not buy another Treasury bond, when the initial bond expired.

After all, if they wanted a long term Treasury bond in the first instance and that product was no longer available the logical decision would be to invest in another bond to enable the desired investment period. This would not increase spending it would merely increase the number of Treasury bond contracts purchased. The emphasis of Demand Fortification is to invest the money in a way that the investment in itself creates aggregate demand. Specifically capital investment in the means of production, such as tools, machinery, factories and training skilled employees which help an economy grow.

Often governments issue debt to pay off existing debt. This action has no effect on capital investment, as it is not used to create output. Unfortunately, this tactic frequently occurs when the economy is in a downturn. As the government has borrowed, the debt has to be paid off. If the form of investment changed, to one that encouraged output for example new business start-ups or existing company expansion. The demand for capital goods and the demand for labour would increase.

The technique of Demand Fortification is to encourage or enforce this type of investment, through incentives or legislation. Some examples of this would be to encourage private sector investment over public sector investment, as public sector investment is often used to pay off existing debt obligations.

Treasury bonds in particular, have been criticised for being a "Ponzi Scheme" (SEC, 2010). Where the investment acts like a pyramid system of payments, with the initial investors receiving the later investors' capital as return until there are no new investors and the fund collapses. If the government continues to borrow more money, to pay off existing debt the market could lose confidence in the government's ability to make future payments.

If this happens, the government will not be able to raise the capital needed to make the debt repayments, or possibly even fail to make payments on the interest of the loan, resulting in default (Mackenzie, 2010). Assuming the repayments are made, they could leave the domestic economy and enter the foreign investor's economy. This will also have a negative consequence to aggregate demand, because a large percentage of the investment governments receive is foreign in origin.

If, both domestic and foreign, investments were made in the private sector, the funds would be used to enable the means of production. Businesses will only borrow money if they have to, due to the cost of the interest charged. Examples of when businesses borrow are to start-up, expand or to pay off short term loans. They also have more means of generating capital than individuals, by issuing equity capital, such as share offerings or partnerships. This is discussed in detail in the "Pecking Order Theory" and is an industry in itself, provided by Corporate Finance companies (Frank & Goyal, 2003).

In addition to the type of investment, the spending habits of the recipient are also important. Smaller businesses, with high resource dependency or labour requirements, such as factories and building companies will have immediate needs to expend capital. Larger businesses or businesses with lower resource dependency and labour requirements, such as consultancies and legal firms will have less immediate needs to expend capital.

By changing the recipients of investments, to the entities with the higher potential need for capital expenditure or those with the more urgent need to use invested money. It could be possible to increase the level of aggregate demand, or conversely taking the opposite action could reduce it (Lumby & Jones, 2003). This could be achieved by reducing Capital Gains Tax on the returns from money invested in the higher capital expenditure entities, or stopping it completely for those investments to entice that direction of lending further.

Another option could be to increase Capital Gains Tax for the entities or investments with the lower capital expenditure, to deter investment in these ventures directing the funds to the higher capital expenditure ventures. This could, in addition provide the government with extra funds to pay off the existing public sector debt. Suggesting it may be the superior option in the current global environment.

The alternative method of achieving the above tactic, to direct investment to the most effective line of use, is to put legislative controls on the investment systems. Quotas of certain types of investments could be introduced, to prevent over investment in low capital expenditure entities. This would likely lead to increased investment in high capital expenditure entities. This may prove unpopular, as it takes away investor freedom and could prevent some businesses from attracting the investment they need to operate effectively. It could also prove difficult to introduce the means necessary to deliver the desired result, due to EU legislation.

One further element of Demand Fortification, which has been touched upon previously in this paper, is the effect of international investment on the domestic level of aggregate demand. The most damaging form of investment to the domestic economy is one that leaves the country, as it plays little if any part in the original country's economy.

A tax reduction on investments that remain in the domestic economy or a tax on foreign investments, could help to prevent capital from leaving the country. Also, investments from foreign economies could be attracted to the domestic economy through incentives such as tax exemptions or trading preferences to bring capital into the country. A stronger position could be set to ban investments outside of the domestic economy, but this is likely to be unpopular and could do damage to international trade and relations.

# Are these tools useful for the ECB and the member states?

These tools are useful and could be used to control the level of aggregate demand, in the member states economies. They eliminate the domestic restraints of aggregate demand control seen in the member states, deriving from private and public sector debt, as they are not based on monetary policy or fiscal policy. They provide a way out of the limitations of the current economic suggestions of money supply theory and practice. However, the criteria and targets of the ECB prohibit the action necessary for the member states to use these techniques. At least in the way needed to resolve their domestic economic problems, as a result of the ECB's prioritisation of the Euro currency value.

The overall health of the Euro currency is put before a member state's domestic economy, creating different requirements for the Eurozone to the individual member states. For example, if the overall Eurozone was over inflated but an individual member state was experiencing deflation. The action taken by the ECB, would counter the action taken by the member state's central bank. If the individual member states were to leave the EU, they would be able to use these tools to the manner they need. Suggesting this may be the only action they can perform.

# Conclusion.

The orthodox tools for controlling aggregate demand are constrained. Partly by the limitations the member states have created and partly by the requirements of the ECB. Monetary policy has been constrained by the overextended private debt market and the tightening credit conditions, that occurred after the subprime mortgage defaults. Fiscal policy has been constrained by the overspending of governments and the political pressures cuts would create, forcing governments to give in to the demands of the masses. The acceptance of economically weak countries into the EU and the Eurozone, have put further pressure on the stability of the overall currency. The criteria of the ECB on both monetary policy and fiscal policy prevents a unified way out.

Member states can control money supply through other means than ECB tools. But at the cost of the primary ECB strategy, of putting the currency value of the Euro before the other aggregate demand requirements of the member states. If member states left the Eurozone, they would not be subject to the restrictions of the ECB and its currency valuation money supply targets. This would enable them to use the alternative aggregate demand control tools to recover from the current economic difficulties. Without the detrimental effects to the money lending market seen with interest rate control or the cost to government deficits seen with fiscal policy control. As the economic situation worsens, this may change from an attractive alternative to the only possibility.

If the ECB continues its stringent control over the member states economies, it can only lead to either economic collapse or the dissolvement of the federal union. If there is a future for the Euro, the weaker member states would have to leave the Eurozone and the wealthier member states would have to concentrate on their own domestic policies. This would include protectionism and the more internal economic policies seen before the Euro's introduction. It is likely that the larger member states, such as Germany and France, would have to resort to cuts in spending and ruthless activities to stop their own economies from deteriorating.

The alternative, if the European single currency is to continue, would be to make radical reforms to the current Eurozone economic governance system. This would include a new prioritisation of aggregate demand control targets, putting domestic member states requirements first. Also, a move to the heterodox aggregate demand controls suggested in this paper would make it easier, if not simply possible, for member states to overcome their monetary and fiscal constraints. If the current private and public debt issues persist, it may be impossible to control aggregate demand in the Eurozone or even in the individual member states using the existing mechanisms.

# Bibliography.

Agrawal, A. (2008, April 17). Retrieved Ocotober 31, 2010, from mostlyeconomics.wordpress.com: http://mostlyeconomics. wordpress.com/2007/10/07/what-is-liquidity/.

Ajuzie, E. (2008). The Quantity Theory of Money Revisited. *Journal of Business and Economics Research*, 125.

Armitstead, L. (2011, June 20). *The Telegraph Finance.* Retrieved January 08, 2012, from The Telegraph: http://www.telegraph.co .uk/finance/financialcrisis/8586852/How-much-could-Britain-pay-to-bail-out-Greece.html.

Barro, R. J. (1996). Reflections on Ricardian Equivalence. *National Bureau of Economic Research*, 1-10.

BBC, N. (2010, April 27). Retrieved May 17, 2010, from news.bbc.co.uk: http://news.bbc.co.uk/1/hi/8647441.stm.

BBC, N. (2012, January 14). *BBC NEWS EUROPE.* Retrieved January 15, 2012, from BBC NEWS: http://www.bbc.co.uk/news /world-europe-16560323.

Beckhart, B. H. (1972). *Federal Reserve System.* Banking Institute and Columbia University Press.

Begg, D., Dornbusch, R. & Fischer, S. (2003). Economics Seventh Edition. Mcgraw-Hill.

Bernanke, B. S., Laubach, T., Mishkin, F. S. & Posen, A. S. (2001). *Inflation Targeting Lessons from the International Experience.* New Jersey: Princeton University Press.

Black, J., Hashimzade, N. & Myles, G. (2009). *Oxford Dictionary of Economics.* Oxford: Oxford University Press.

Branson, W. H. (1989). *Macroeconomics Theory and Policy, Third Edition.* New York: Harper & Row.

Brealey, R. A. & Myers, S. C. (2003). Principles of Corporate Finance Seventh Edition. Mcgraw-Hill.

Buiter, W. (2008, December 9). Retrieved November 1, 2010, from blogft.com: http://blogs.ft.com/maverecon/2008/12/ quantitative-easing-and-qualitative-easing-a-terminological- and-taxonomic-proposal/.

Congdon, T. (2009). *Central Banking in a Free Society.* London: IEA.

Davies, L., Lowes, B. & Pass, C. L. (2005). Collins Dictionary of Economics, 4th edition. Publisher. HarperCollins, Glasgow 2005.

Dixon, H. & Hadas, E. (2009, January 1). Retrieved May 20, 2010, from www.nytimes.com: http://www.nytimes.com/2009/01/11 /business/worldbusiness/11iht-views12.1.19248009.html.

Dunai, M. (2010, October 26). Retrieved October 27, 2010, from www.forexpros.com: http://www.forexpros.com/news/interest -rates-news/factbox-pension-schemes-across-central-eastern- europe-169221.

EC. (2010, January 8). Retrieved May 17, 2010, from epp.eurostat.ec.europa.eu: http://appsso.eurostat.ec.europa.eu/nui /show.do?dataset=gov_dd_edpt1&lang=en.

ECB. (2010). Retrieved May 10, 2010, from www.ecb.int: http:// www.ecb.int/mopo/intro/html/index.en.html.

Euronews. (2011, December 11). Retrieved January 08, 2012, from Euro News: http://www.euronews.net/2011/12/11/eu-treaty-veto-causes-rift-in-uk-coalition/.

Europa. (2010). Retrieved May 17, 2010, from www.europa.eu: http://europa.eu/scadplus/glossary/convergence_criteria_en. Htm.

Eurostat. (2010, April 24). Retrieved May 17, 2010, from epp.eurostat.ec.europa.eu: http://appsso.eurostat.ec.europa.eu/nui /show.do?dataset=gov_dd_edpt1&lang=en.

Frank, M. Z. & Goyal, V. K. (2003). Testing the Pecking Order Theory of Capital Structure. *Journal of Financial Economics*, 1-10.

George, E. (2003). *Montrans pdf*. Retrieved October 25, 2010, from http://www.bankofengland.co.uk/publications/other/ monetary/montrans.pdf.

Grice, A. (2009, December 4). Retrieved May 20, 2010, from www.independent.co.uk: http://www.independent.co.uk/news /uk/politics/163850bn-official-cost-of-the-bank-bailout-1833830.html.

Heritage, T. (2010, April 26). Retrieved May 20, 2010, from
uk.reuters.com: http://uk.reuters.com/article/idUKTRE63O0R7201
00426.

Hewitt, G. (2011, December 09). *BBC NEWS POLITICS*. Retrieved
January 08, 2012, from BBC NEWS: http://www.bbc.co.uk/news
/uk-16104275.

HM Revenue & Customs. (2010). *HMRC*. Retrieved October 25,
2010, from http://www.hmrc.gov.uk/stats/pensions/table7-
9.pdf.

IASIE, I. A. (1987). Retrieved October 25, 2010, from
www.genevaassociation.org: http://www.genevaassociation.org/
Research_Programme/Four_Pillars_Pensions.aspx.

IMF. (2010). *Greece: Staff Report on Request for Stand-By
Arrangement IMF Country Report No. 10/110*. Washington, D.C.:
© 2010 International Monetary Fund.

Investopedia. (2010, October 30). Retrieved October 30, 2010,
from www.investopedia.com: http://www.investopedia.com/
terms/p/pump-priming.asp.

Investors, A. G. (2010). Retrieved October 25, 2010, from
www.pensionfundsonline.co.uk: http://www.pensionfundsonline.co.
uk/countryprofiles/hungary.aspx.

Jones, L. (2010, May 21). Retrieved October 31, 2010, from
www.moneymarketing.com: http://www.moneymarketing.co.
uk/investments/news/is-global-deflation-being-overlooked?/
1012164.article.

Krugman, P. R. & Obstfeld. M. (2003) International Economics: Theory and Policy Sixth Edition. Pearson Education.

Leigh, C. (2010). Retrieved October 25, 2010, from www.whenigrowrich.co.uk: http://www.whenigrowrich.co.uk/corp/stakepen.htm.

Lumby, S. & Jones, C. (2003). Corporate Finance Theory & Practice Seventh Edition. Thomson.

Mackenzie, M. (2010, October 29). Retrieved November 1, 2010, from www.ft.com: http://www.ft.com/cms/s/0/83307ab2-e382-11df-8ad3-00144feabdc0,s01=1.html?ftcamp=rss.

McDowell, D. (2010, May 6). Retrieved October 28, 2010, from www.worldpoliticsreview.com: http://www.worldpoliticsreview.com/articles/5502/greek-debt-crisis-and-the-piigs-europes-financial-swine-flu.

MENAFN. (2010, March 21). Retrieved May 20, 2010, from www.menafn.com: http://www.menafn.com/qn_news_story_s.asp?StoryId=1093315566.

Nadeau, R. (2008, 21 August). Retrieved October 30, 2010, from www.eoearth.org: http://www.eoearth.org/article/Neoclassical_economic_theory.

Palley, T. I. (2007, February 23-25). Retrieved October 31, 2010, from www.thomaspalley.com: http://www.thomaspalley.com/docs/research/macro_monetary.pdf.

Peston, R. (2011, October 10). *BBC NEWS POLITICS.* Retrieved January 09, 2012, from BBC NEWS: http://www.bbc.co.uk/news/business-15235915.

Rahman, M. P. (2010, October 26). Retrieved October 27, 2010, from www.morganstanley.com: http://www.morganstanley.com/views/gef/index.html.

Schuman, M. (2011, July 22). *The Curious Capitalist*. Retrieved January 08, 2012, from http://curious capitalist.blogs.time.com/2011/07/22/will-the-second-greek-bailout-save-the-euro/.

Sciolino, E. & Smith, C. S. (2006, March 29). Retrieved October 28, 2010, from www.nytimes.com: http://www.nytimes.com/2006/03/29/international/europe/29france.html.

SEC, U. S. (2010, November 1). Retrieved November 2010, 2010, from www.sec.gov: http://www.sec.gov/answers/ponzi.htm.

Stein, J. L. (1981). *Monetarist, Keynesian, and New Classical Economics*. American Economics Association.

Stewart, H. (2009, January 29). Retrieved October 28, 2010, from www.guardian.co.uk: http://www.guardian.co.uk/business/2009/jan/29/question-and-answer-quantitative-easing.

TPAS, T. P. (2010). Retrieved October 27, 2010, from www.pensionadvisoryservice.org.uk: http://www.pensionsadvisoryservice.org.uk/workplace-pension-schemes/final-salary-schemes/avcs.

Tyldesley, H. (2010, April 29). Retrieved May 17, 2010, from news.sky.com.

Zaretsky, A. M. (2008). Retrieved November 1, 2010, from acheson.files.wordpress.com: http://acheson.files.wordpress.com/2008/03/operationtwist.pdf.

# Appendix I.

|      | Euro Area (16 States) | Greece |
|------|-----------------------|--------|
| 2000 | 0                     | -3.7   |
| 2001 | -1.9                  | -4.7   |
| 2002 | -2.6                  | -4.8   |
| 2003 | -3.1                  | -5.6   |
| 2004 | -2.9                  | -7.5   |
| 2005 | -2.5                  | -5.2   |
| 2006 | -1.3                  | -3.6   |
| 2007 | -0.6                  | -5.1   |
| 2008 | -0.2                  | -7.7   |
| 2009 | -6.3                  | -13.6  |

Table 1 (Eurostat, 2010).

Euro Area and Greek public sector deficits for the years

2000 - 2009.

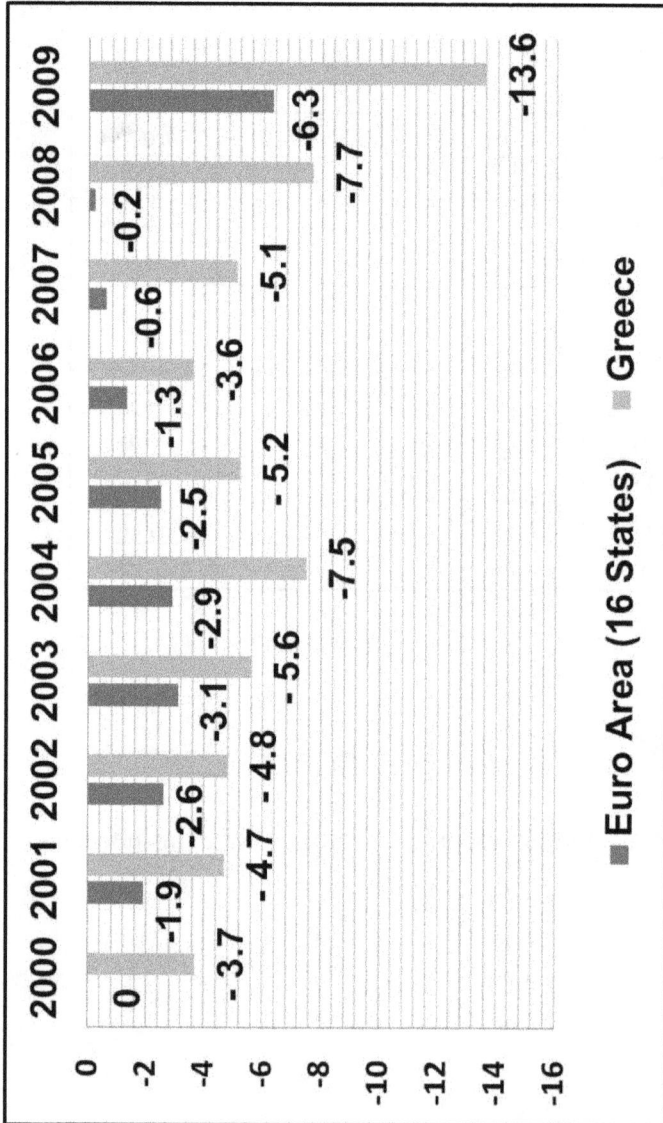

Graph 1 (Eurostat, 2010). Showing Euro Area and Greek public sector deficits for the years 2000 - 2009 from Table 1.

| | 2000 | 2001 | 2002 | 2003 | 2004 | 2005 | 2006 | 2007 | 2008 | 2009 |
|---|---|---|---|---|---|---|---|---|---|---|
| Euro Area | 0.0 | -1.9 | -2.6 | -3.1 | -2.9 | -2.5 | -1.3 | -0.6 | -2.0 | -6.3 |
| Greece | -3.7 | -4.5 | -4.8 | -5.6 | -7.5 | -5.2 | -3.6 | -5.1 | -7.7 | -13.6 |
| Latvia (NEZ) | -2.8 | -2.1 | -2.3 | -1.6 | -1.0 | -0.4 | -0.5 | -0.3 | -4.1 | -9.0 |
| Lithuania (NEZ) | -3.2 | -3.6 | -1.9 | -1.3 | -1.5 | -0.5 | -0.4 | -1.0 | -3.3 | -8.9 |
| Hungary | -3.0 | -4.0 | -8.9 | -7.2 | -6.4 | -7.9 | -9.3 | -5.0 | -3.8 | -4.0 |
| Malta | -6.2 | -6.4 | -5.5 | -9.8 | -4.7 | -2.9 | -2.6 | -2.2 | -4.5 | -3.8 |
| Poland (NEZ) | -3.0 | -5.3 | -5.0 | -6.2 | -5.4 | -4.1 | -3.6 | -1.9 | -3.7 | -7.1 |
| Slovenia | -3.7 | -4.0 | -2.5 | -2.7 | -2.2 | -1.4 | -1.3 | 0.0 | -1.7 | -5.5 |
| Slovakia | -12.3 | -6.5 | -8.2 | -2.8 | -2.4 | -2.8 | -3.5 | -1.9 | -2.3 | -6.8 |

Table 2 (Eurostat, 2010). Euro Area and struggling member states public sector deficits for the years 2000 - 2009.

NEZ = None Euro Zone.

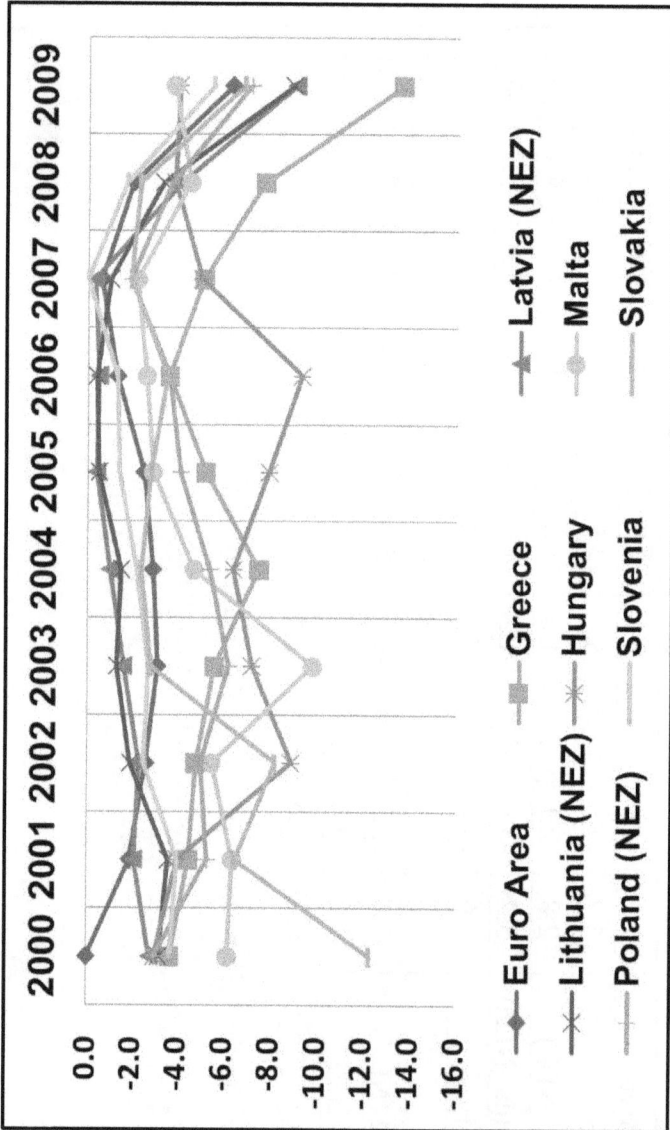

Graph 2 (Eurostat, 2010). Showing Euro Area and struggling member states public sector deficits for the years 2000 - 2009 from Table 2.

# Appendix III.

|  | Average | SDEV |
|---|---|---|
| Euro Area (16 States) | -2.32 | 1.71 |
| Greece | -6.13 | 2.96 |
| Latvia (NEZ) | -2.41 | 2.61 |
| Lithuania (NEZ) | -2.56 | 2.51 |
| Hungary | -5.95 | 2.29 |
| Malta | -4.86 | 2.26 |
| Poland (NEZ) | -4.53 | 1.56 |
| Slovenia | -2.5 | 1.57 |
| Slovakia | -4.95 | 3.4 |

Table 3 (Eurostat, 2010).

Euro Area and struggling member states mean averages and

standard deviations of public sector deficits for the years

2000 - 2009.

NEZ = None Euro Zone.

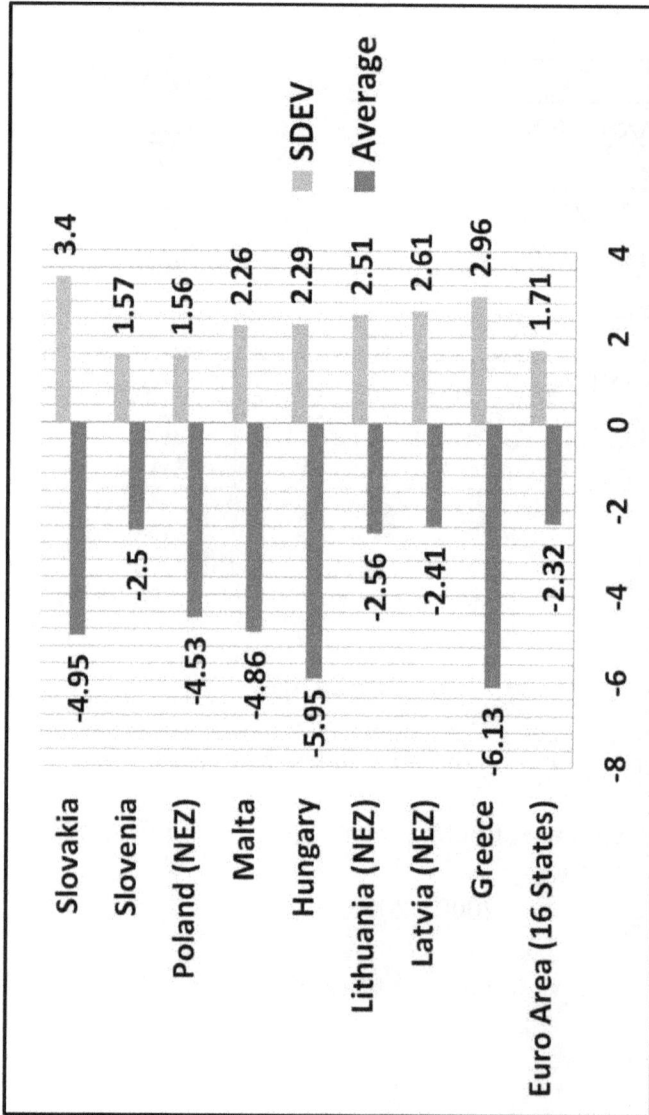

Graph 3 (Eurostat, 2010). Showing Euro Area and struggling member states mean averages and standard deviations of public sector deficits for the years 2000 - 2009 from Table 3.

# Appendix IV.

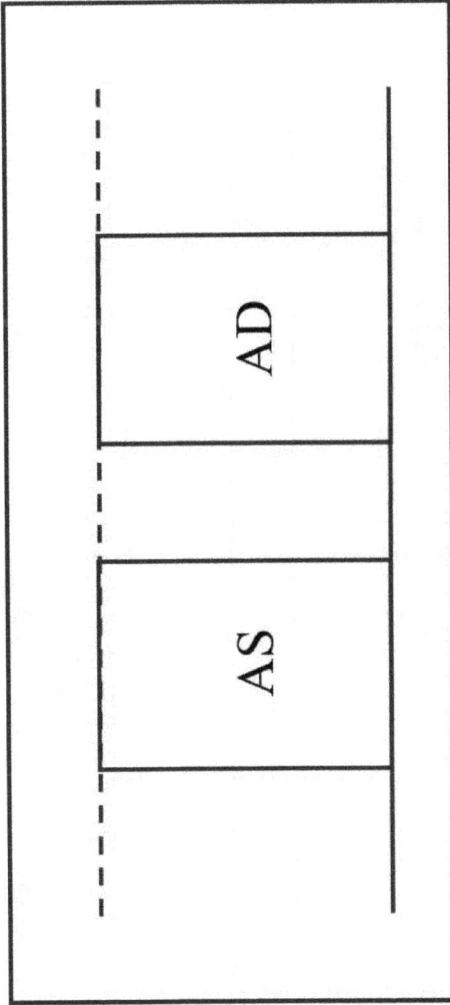

Diagram 1. Equilibrium.

AS = Aggregate Supply.          AD = Aggregate Demand.

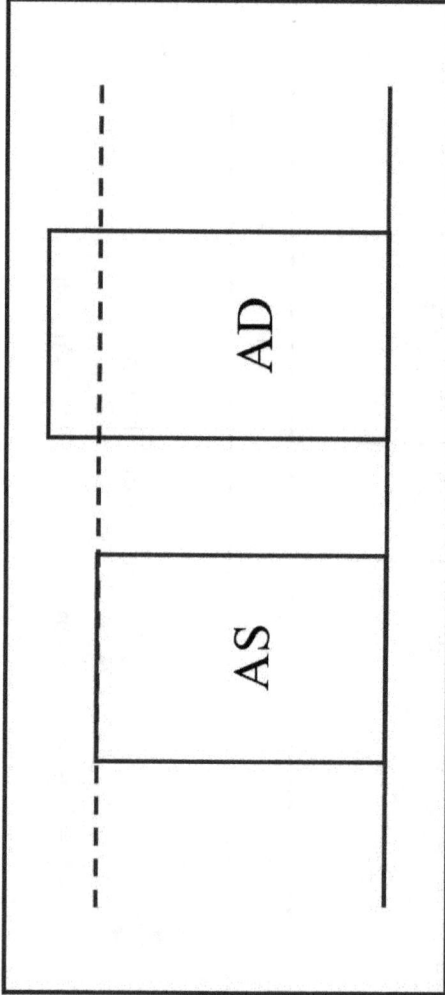

Diagram 2. Inflation.

AS = Aggregate Supply.    AD = Aggregate Demand.

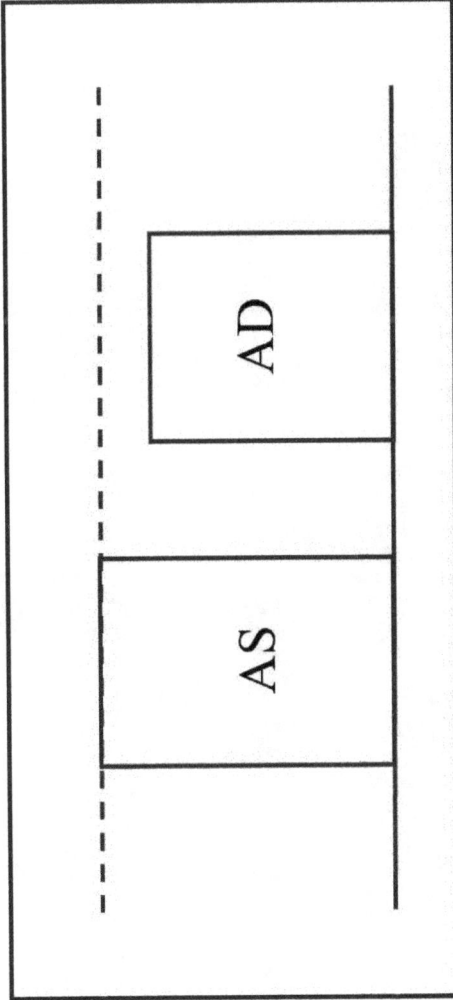

Diagram 3. Deflation.

AS = Aggregate Supply.          AD = Aggregate Demand.

# Appendix V.

An example of the practical application of liquidity efficiency.

Assume that an economy has consumption made up of a third income from people who have a high propensity to consume, a third income from people who have a medium propensity to consume and a third income from people who have a low propensity to consume.

To maximise the efficiency of the liquidity, the liquidity has to be transformed from having a large proportion of its composition from the lower consuming members of society to having a greater proportion of its composition from the higher consuming members of society.

Now assume that the liquidity can be broken up into units. To work out the liquidity efficiency of each of these units use the formula below. When Y = Income, C = The percentage of the income that is consumed (propensity to consume), TR = Transactions and E = C divided by 100.

Y x E = TR

For example;

Y = £1,000

C = 80%

£1,000 x 0.8 = £800.

Now suppose that the income for everyone in this economy is equal (although this is not likely, the whole point of this example is to explain how different people have different incomes and different propensities to consume), to simplify the concept, but they have different propensities to consume one third is 90%, another third is 70% and the final third is only 20%.

If we then work out the actual levels of consumption in terms of the monetary units used in the economy over a specific period of time, it will demonstrate how advantageous liquidity efficiency can be. Each of the three sectors (or thirds) who consume in this example will have an income of £1,000 per month and the example will be over an annual period, so the total of the formula will have to be multiplied by 12.

As the same income has been paid to all sectors of the society, it will demonstrate the actual consumption that each sector of the society will generate (please note it is unlikely that people will have different propensities to consume if they have the same income. It is understood that if a person's income changes it will alter their propensity to consume, this is just a very simple model to explain the concept of liquidity efficiency).

The sector with 90% propensity to consume;

£1,000 x 0.9 = £900.          £900 x 12 = £10,800.

This sector will consume £10,800 out of the £12,000 that they will receive in income.

The sector with 70% propensity to consume;

£1,000 x 0.7 = £700.                £700 x 12 = £8,400.

This sector will consume £8,400 out of the £12,000 that they will receive in income.

The sector with 20% propensity to consume;

£1,000 x 0.2 = £200.                £200 x 12 = £2,400.

This sector will consume £2,400 out of the £12,000 that they will receive in income.

If the sector with the 20% propensity to consume was taxed more in a way that it reduced their income by £200 per month, the annual reduction in consumption would be.

£800 x 0.20 = £160.                £160 x 12 = £1,920.

£2,400 - £1,920 = £480.

The annual reduction in consumption is £480.

If the sector with the 90% propensity to consume was taxed less in a way that it increased their income by £200 per month, the annual increase in consumption would be.

£1,200 x 0.90 = £1,080.        £1,080 x 12 = £12,960.

£12,960 - £10,800 = £2,160.

The annual increase in consumption is £2,160.

£2,160 - £480 = £1,680.

By transferring the £200 per month from the sector with the lower propensity to consume to the sector with the higher propensity to consume, £480 in consumption is lost but £2,160 in consumption is gained. Overall consumption has increased by £1,680.

£1,680 / £480 = 3.5.

By transferring £200 of income a month from the sector with the 20% propensity to consume to the sector with the 90% propensity to consume, the £200 is now producing 3.5 times more consumption. The level of aggregate demand has increased without impacting interest rates or tax intake.

But what impact has this had on the total level of aggregate demand. If we add up all of the consumption figures for the pre £200 transfer, first, example;

£10,800 + £8,400 + £2,400 = £21,600 consumption.

If we add up all of the consumption figures for the post £200 transfer, second, example;

£12,960 + £8,400 + £1,920 = £23,280 consumption.

£23,280 - £21,600 = £1,680.

(£1,680 / £21,600) x 100 = 7.777%.

The efficiency of the income liquidity has increased by 7.777% without altering tax intake.

**Alternative Economics.**
Morganist Economics
Perspectives Volume I.

**Description.** A compilation
of articles, essays and concepts
of the Morganist School of
Economic Thought.
**ISBN 978-1-62407-489-9.**

**Modern Applied Macroeconomics.**

**Description.** A Conceptual and Technical
Paper, Putting Forward Pension and
Economic Reforms.
**ISBN 978-1-5136-4833-0.**

**Economic Growth.**
In a Highly Constrained Environment.

**Description.** New Techniques and
Alternative Governmental Dynamics
to Enable Economic Growth.
**ISBN 978-1-5136-5076-0.**

**Available at leading online book retailers.**

## Notes.

www.ingramcontent.com/pod-product-compliance
Lightning Source LLC
Chambersburg PA
CBHW031813190326
41518CB00006B/322